C000134143

*Hope that you enjoy, guys.*

*Xxx*

True cure

Depression:
Suppression;
Shame,
Pain,
Twisted notions and ideas.
Results from our need for approval in our fears
and our craving.
Self harming,
Desperate and holding on too tight.
Searching for way out; Searching for the light,
Terrified!!!
Too cold, too sensitive,
Neglected.
Misunderstood,
Low worth,
Scarred,
Drained,
Unbalanced brain!
Feel too much then too little,
Unstable.
Overridden with It all!
Anorexia,
Bipolar ... Etc.
All similar.
All In need of some type of drug...
The only true cures are compassion and love!!!

# Home

In the wilderness, I wonder majestically.
I am free. Belonging wherever my wings may
fall.
Like an eagle, but still as grounded as a tree.
For, unlike a home, this is my true soul's
sanctuary. The place in which I feel safe, and
where my heart longs to be. For, it is here that,
in peace and awareness, I have full
understanding of reality. Escaping all that I may
question, or what may burden me. I roam to
find truth & my true home!

Birth of purity

From my room, I peer out the
window; Onto the trees
and blooming roses below. As
the sun rises and a new day
begins; The first day of Spring.
Up here the sky is brighter.
The air fresh and my mind
lighter. From my window, and
room's sanctuary, there is
deeper clarity. Not long having
risen from hibernation.
For, with my arms out
stretched, I embrace and
welcome
the new season!

Where the heart resides

To old familiar places pieces of my heart stay,
as well as stray,
Whenever I'm lost and can't find my way.
Each representing a different chapter and a
lesson,
That I reminisce and contemplate In.
Stories told
From the familiar and the old;
Haunts my soul,
The past that I hold.
What made me the person whom I came to
be,
And of whom reminds me.
Locked In my heart and stored In my memory.
And is what, too, haunts these places; My soul,
spirit and energy.

Butterfly

Their array of colours
illuminates the sky.
Like a flower that has took to
flight; Sailing near & high,
Making the days more bright.
Fluttering their wings so
effortlessly & elegantly,
Unlike the bee, whose
movement is brisk & direct.
They escape their cocoon,
with their wings freely out
stretched.
Mesmerizing onlookers as they
dance & twirl.
Circling the ground,
like fairy ballerinas; Embracing
each Summer & Spring,
And scattering splendour &
beauty all around!

# Glaciers of her heart

Surrounded by the Atlantic ocean & night's sky, she finds herself on an island made out of vast Glaciers of ice.
By the gentle glow of the lanterns she is enticed,
Up the steps of her awareness,
Towards a beautiful, flowing spring; In it's tepidness she merges.
Bathing in and soaking up her potential, she feels replenished & revitalized,
And more aware & open are her eyes.
She then travels down the steps;
Back to the Artic world of her depths.
Absent from the warmth of the spring, she finds herself extra sensitive to her bitter harsh, atmosphere.
And, bare footed, feels the hard, frozen, rigidness of the ice beneath her.
No sooner, she is mysteriously clothed in a white robe and slippers,
Mirroring her glistening surrounds, as well as the distant crowd of strangers.
For, in their presence she feels wary,
And desperately tries to seek out something that's familiar and homely,
But instead, still guided by the lights, she is led nearer to where they are settled; Gathered Inside a small tavern, chatting and joking freely.
The barmaid acknowledges her. "Come and have a drink", she utters warmly.
She hesitates but, overcome by tiredness and thirst, she accepts her invitation. Resting at the bar, her hostility begins to lighten,
And her fear & panic is replaced with a sense of harmony and union,
As she mingles with the crowd. Eventually, feeling completely relaxed, she lets go,
Causing the ice beneath her to crack and give way, melting the Glaciers of her heart's dwelling.
Creating more oceans, rivers and springs, In which, like it's plants and life, she can too flourish and grow!

Happiness

When it comes to finding
happiness I don't
have to search too far, and
have discovered
it in the smallest and
simplest of things.

But what makes us more
humble,
and able to experience ALL
of the pleasures that life
brings!

The final
voyage

Waiting to board, In the confinements of his cabin, the Captain sat sheepishly. And, In no hurry, rested, between the hours of carrying luggage down onto harbour,
In preparation for his next journey; Taking care not to Include any unnecessarily baggage and clutter.
Before witnessing and part-taking in battle with the people below. As they launched their missiles, not only at each other but at him also, while he stood in the middle;
Motionless & still. Eventually, they were led onto individual ships,
Where they continued to battle, amongst the vast Atlantic. Those on his side he sailed alongside, in the same direction, And, together, shot the enemies, without hesitation;
Flipping their ships upside down. Until, one by-one, they drowned! Victorious, the Captain's ship was then cleansed, and in it he began to ascend; Weightlessly sailing across the skies, on his way to his next, new adventure & final voyage!

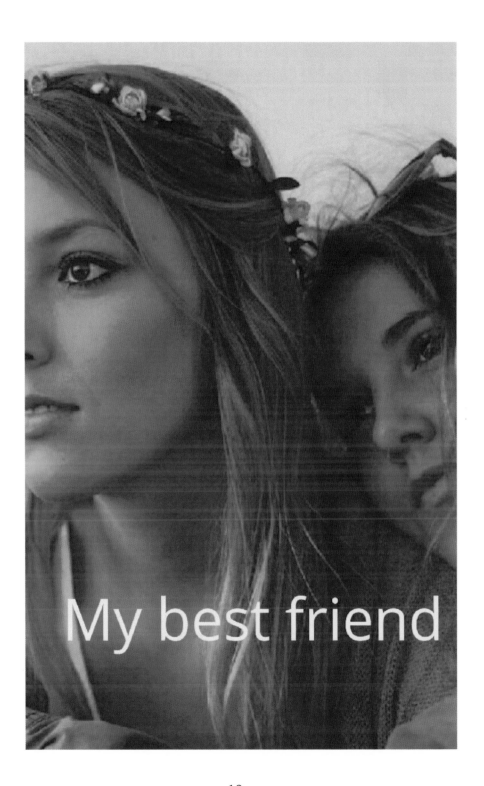

My best friend

She is more brutally honest than
anyone. But whose advice I
cherish the most. And to whom I
share a bond, that's so strong,
That compared to others doesn't
come close.
She knows me better than anyone,
Including all of my imperfections
and flaws! Yet who loves
and accepts me just as I am;
Without justification or cause.
When I'm feeling down, She lifts me
like no
other. She is, without doubt, my true
best friend,
And my mother!

Baptism by fire

It was in a firey cave that to new life
she gave birth;
Away from society, hidden beneath
the earth.
Whilst, still, to the world she
maintained a connection,
As, within herself, of her strength she
had recognition,
As well as her power, that generated
within the scorching heat of the fire.
At peace, in the cave; The doorway to
her soul, she sought shelter.
While too, in the flames, she was
purified,
Then baptised.

The greater the curse

From her window, she gazed into the deep;
First at the stars, then beyond them she began to seek.
In search of what? She could not say?
But her heart was open.
And In wonder she found freedom.
Though she was also naive in her youth.
Not yet corrupted, her soul was pure,
Carrying light, compassion & truth.
It wasn't long until, by her light, darkness was lured. For, without it's luminosity it knew it could not prevail.
The more open her heart was so too was the greater the curse
& the spell!

Let the sun shine in

In the Summer the birds sing and
rejoice.
Leafs begin to dance around with the
gentle, calm breeze.
Flowers, after months of hiding, open
their petals, as
if to welcome the glistening heavens,
And reach far and wide towards the
sky.

Beauty only forms from Winter's
darkness
when you embrace the Sunshine,
And your spirits are high.

# A knight's stiring

In exasperation, I stand on the veranda & gaze far out into
the deep
&, distracted in thought, I meditate,
Sipping my whisky, as I feel the scorch of the slates beneath
my bare feet.
Not long before I had vowed to rest, but remain awake,
After the sun had bidden me good night, & the heavens had
gone to sleep.
For, all is quiet & seemingly peaceful, yet inside I am moved
&
stirred,
Like the rising of the atmosphere...
For, someplace cooler I long to fleet.
All of a sudden all is no longer calm,
As I hear a loud roar coming from above, as if the heavens
had too been aroused by an Alarm...
Then the clouds, like two knights with swords on horses,
across the sky ride,
& suddenly into each other they crash!
I continue to watch as, within the sky's depths, by the
thunder, I see light at last. No sooner the heavens open their
gates,
& the downpour I embrace. And, feeling cleansed, I am no
longer in longing and in search of the days gone past.

Lion's View

Like Africa's Safaris & Jungles,
Lost, she stands in the mist of vast, endless
fields.

Soon, she senses that she is not alone,
&, in the distance, catches sight of a predator.
As it, upon awakening, begins to roam.

Fearful, she turns frozen and still,
As the lions stalks her path, in search of a
meal.

It stops & gazes at her,
Then slowly approaches further near.

She runs,
without checking whether she's being chased,
& climbs a hill where, at the very top, she feels
safe.

Gradually, like an expert hunter, her vision
expands;
All the fields & beyond she can then see clear.

And no longer feels fear,
As she glances at the lion below;
That is her true self, strength & ego!

# Preacher

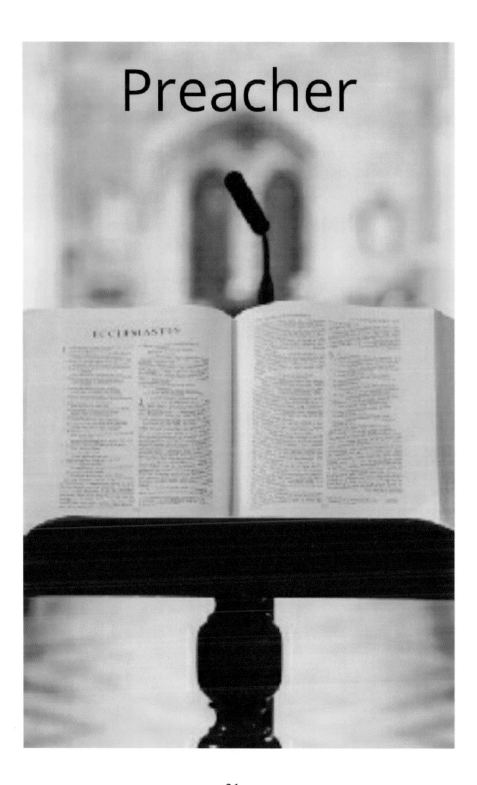

There once lived a man who loved
to preach,
But, with his words, he could not
reach,
Until his podium, on which he
stood, crumbled and, from his
stature, he fell, and amongst the
people he began to dwell.
Bringing too the crashing of his
beliefs, but with it bringing fourth
truth, which ultimately brought him
to knees!

# Waterfall

In nature's sereneness
there's much beauty,
Which can alleviate you
when you're tense &
feeling
low. Like a waterfall, with
it's rejuvenating downfall.
Which, rather than
fighting, surrenders to
the
current
& goes with the flow!

Fly or die

I rose from the bottom, now I stand on the top of the
cliffs.
My vision no longer restricted;
High enough to see what is below and what is before
me.
I gaze into the clear sea,
Where I witness much life.
By it's shimmering waters I am enticed.

All of a sudden, I find myself distracted by a flock of
birds near by;
How like them I long to fly.
Though am aware that I could instead fall and die.

Yet my fear is over ridden
With drive and determination,
As well as a deep yearning in which to live.
In my heart I know there is no other way;
On these cliffs I can not stay.
I have to take the risk.

For, either way I don't exist!
All baggage I leave, so that I am light,
As I prepare for my flight.
To this life I say farewell and goodbye.
And, expanding my wings, I reach towards the sky!

Rise

There once lived a young Lioness, who dreamt of climbing one particular tree in her forest. To rise to it's very top was her hearts request. Although among her siblings she was the smallest. And of all the trees that stood in the forest it was the tallest. But she was young and had no fear. Yet naive to the danger ... As the branch snapped from the tree she tumbled. Wounded, she lay on the ground, as, above her, the vultures circled ... Then, scoping down, into her they tore. She cried out from the agony of their sharp teeth & claws. Enraged, she began to fight back, with all of her might. Until, one by one, they cowered, and quickly to safety she neared. With a damaged leg, her dream of climbing that tree she had to forget, and, living in the wild, in it's place, gradually she found herself burdened with many other hardships. She continued to prowl that same forest as a decade passed through time. Then one day upon a different, much younger, tree she stumbled; Nestled amongst the vine, in which she decided to climb. No longer a tiny cub, she was prevailing in stature and in her prime. Skilfully searching the grounds for hidden prey, from it's very top, she peered down onto the tree of which heights she had once aspired. As well as all the others in the forest, which she had exceeded and soared. For, much more strong and wise, above all she had managed to rise. And she smiled
as, in the distance, from it's heights, she caught sight of her pride!

Free spirit

In the cool, open Summer air, she cycled down the lane from her home
to a destination unknown. Though, soon, she became lost & upon a strange
house she stumbled.
It was small, yet felt inviting, warm & humble.
So through It's front door she ventured, without knocking;
Leading her right through the living room and into the kitchen.
However, not long after, she found herself locked in.
Panicked, she called for help, but the house was bare;
With no one except her there!
The only exit was through a tunnel.
On the other side was the outdoor sunlight;
Reflecting off it's glass & dazzling her with it's bright light. However, it's
opening was too small,
As she discovered while she tried to climb in; Lowering herself onto the
floor, upon opening it's multi-coloured, mosaic glass door.
Minutes turned to hours, &, feeling isolated, she tried to make the place
more pleasing & familiar;
Moving around the bits of furniture.
Till, on the couch, she sat a while & rested;
Drained & exhausted,
Then began to write in a diary.
Though, belonging to the house's owner and not to her, she erased &
rewrote the passages in its pages.
All of a sudden, she was startled by the sound of the turning of a key. It was
the house's occupant; A youngish looking lady.
She kindly offered to give her a lift home. Although she was lost, the lady,
seemed to know the way, despite herself being a little weary,
As she too had claimed to have had trouble travelling through the same
lanes earlier on that day ...
On her arrival home, out the back door & onto the path she wandered
eagerly; Surrounded by the vast ocean sea.
Taking in & exhaling the fresh, crisp, salty air, she finally, at last, felt
free, and glanced out at the tide, & at the wave raring near,
Although, of it, she had no fear,
And held her head high; Keeping it afloat the water,
Unlike the last time, when she went under,
Letting the wave wash over her.
And, cleansed, she was ready to start anew; Having, from her prison, she had
discovered & released a part of herself that she never before knew!

Beggar man

"Oh, what a poor, hard-done-
by man am I".
Were his thoughts, as
he roamed in the bitter
coldness, in which he
thrived.
Yet was never satisfied;
Hungry by a longing
restlessness inside.
So he remained hollow;
Eaten up until bitterness was
all that he could swallow.
In the end he cried,
And, as usual, in his
bitterness, longed to feel
alive.
Yet died.

Revived

Alone on the shore, I peer out to sea; At the tide.
Breathing In deep, I take In It's beauty;
Hearing nothing but the seagulls and the sound of the waves when I close my eyes.
Emptying my mind, I begin to relax and unwind,
As, feeling at peace, with the ocean I become one,
And with It's surrounding nature Intertwined.
Lowering my body onto the sand, I say good night with the setting sun.
For the tide to set I await patiently;
Willing and ready.
For It's warm blanket to tuck me In, cleanse and wash over me,
Before setting me free...
Glancing up, I see the wave raring near,
But am absent of fear.
Aware that Into the ocean's depths I will be carried down,
But I know, for, I will not drown!
Rather, I will be revived, as I'm carried back to shore;
Emerging more alive than before!

# Valley of strength

Sensing my fear, in the darkness, I feel you near...
As, searching for the light, inside of me hopelessness
you ignite.
Before me, in the distance, I see a mysterious glow ...
A pinpoint of fire? Feeling like a prisoner, I command
you to release me!
But you just laugh, as the flames dance and roar;
Stretching taller and opening and revealing what
appears to be a secret door ...
"Granted", you then reply. "I'll set you free".
You then point towards the door. "Behind this light is even
greater than before. Hurry now! Don't hesitate, or I'll make
you my whore"!
The Surrounding blackness thickens, rendering me completely
blind.
Fearful, I worry that I'm running out of time!
Then too does the air, till I can breath no more, as by it's
intense
weight,
I'm weighed to the floor.
In desperation, I glance at the door ...
"Come towards my light. Come now, my child.
I'll see that you're alright"...
But your beckoning I ignore,
As inside I am overcome by a peaceful calm. And instead I
listen to
my inner voice;
Assuring me that I can, and shall, win this war!!! Then even in
your darkness I begin to see. Suddenly the air lightens and I
rise,
As you vanish before me!

# Summer of her bloom

At the festival, as day turned to night,
she celebrated. To the beats & rhythms of
the music, amongst the lights & crowd, she danced.
Before her, in the open air, she gazed upon a stage,
that was illuminated. Pinned to her chest, she clutched
her
gold broach,
of which she was reminded. Then smiled confidently;
Feeling high, yet grounded, and in control, yet uninhibited.

Suddenly she was more aware of the field, by which
she was surrounded,
As she, within her surroundings, felt more relaxed &
connected. Slowly, away from the crowd & nearer to the
stage she edged; Ready to stand unattended. Her true self
& nature she embraced, within the field's more open,
wide
spaces. And, from the seeds that she had planted, her
dreams she could then harvest.

# Spirit of the storm

Her life felt like an endless storm of destruction & chaos,
In which she'd mourn,
for the wasted dreams & years that she had lost.
Fearing it was too late, as, trapped within the storm,
there seemed to be no escape.
Though she never completely gave up the fight for it to end.
However, the more she fought the weaker she felt, thus the
more energy
from her it would take, and further into the madness she would
descend!
Within her mind, body & spirit there was never any lasting rest
or peace, so she remained awake.
Like the petals of a flower, by the hurling winds, she was blown,
pushed & lifted from one stage of despair to the next.
Overwhelmed, she became like a ghost; Subdued. As within
the different stages she dwelled, anxiety crept;
A growing pressure building up inside,
That kept the storm alive.
A storm, from which she could not run from or hide.
But then, like the wind, by which it was created, with the storm
she suddenly danced & twirled,
Until, like her, finally it settled.
On the ground the atmosphere then lifted & became lighter, as
she became healed!

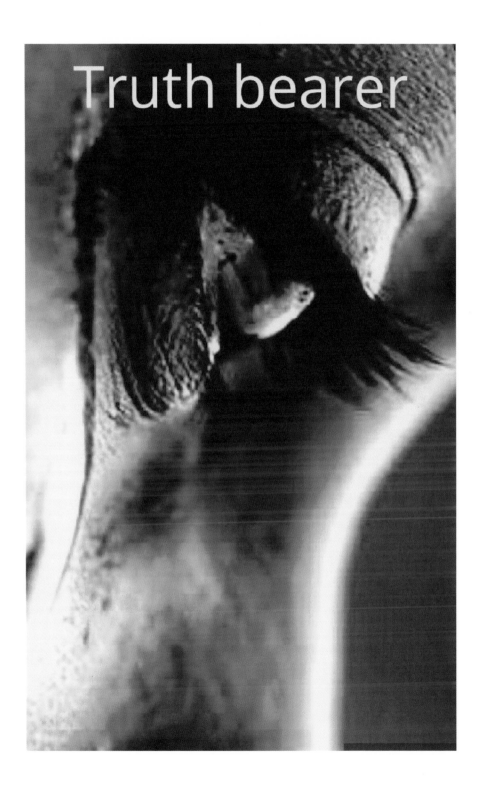

Truth bearer

Being nothing more than a mere prisoner of his past
he was reminded,
As with It's darkness on a daily basis he became reacquainted.
Unwilling and unable to face the clear light of the present day.
With everything laid out before him he turned his back and
walked away!
Reality too painful,
And it's truth, which left him unstable; Cold and hard, with no
crystal
ball in sight. Or magic wand to make everything right!
Continually leading him back, stumbling and falling, down the
path
of his past, where in it's shadows he strayed.
And, too, where his demons silently lay;
Unchained and untamed,
As they fed on his sorrow and his pain.
Sobbing and Flying into uncontrollable rages,
His diary with unsent letters pleading for answers he took and
tore
up it's pages! Ashamed, behind buildings, he tried to hide.
But, still, could not escape from the demons that lurked Inside!
As their claws proceeded to, like knives, cut and pierce him deep,
Causing him to cry out In unbearable pain, and his flesh to
weep!
Until, defeated, on the muddy ground, he began to kneel;
Grasping at the grass and the soil.
For, It was then that, in those dark hours, he began to heal.
As his broken heart and torn soul he cradled,
Down on him the sun gazed.
With the past gradually laid to rest and buried,
Of It he became free,
Bringing forth growth for brighter days; Fresh and new.
After, In his heart, he felt the truth that, in his mind, he
already knew!

Perfection

Perfection ...
What is it's true definition?
Like beauty, is it only a matter of
perception?
And opinion?
I believe so, and that it exists In all of
creation.
For, when you
gaze deeper, and beyond destruction,
Without judgement or discrimination,
You will discover meaning and worth,
Like in the making of our Universe!

Shattered faith

Up and down the same old road, he wandered;
Destitute and penniless.
Exhausted, yet restless.
At night, in a broken down and derelict church he sheltered.
For, his life and reality was one in which he would have rather
not existed,
And, so rather slowly sank further into madness.
Trapped and enthralled, he was a prisoner on the road on
which he
drifted. With neither a present nor
a future; The road that led him to his past, where he
sheepishly
pondered.
Like the church in which, amongst it's ruins, he lay so too was
his
faith shattered and his heart broken.
By night, tired, he, at last, rested, and dreamt of the past,
But no more with sadness in his expression. While, in his
hand, he
clutched a photograph of his wife and children, going back to
the
time before the day of that fateful collision.
Then suddenly he was awoken.
Cradling his chest, in submission, he was overcome by his
burden
& his grief.
And, hands clasped, was weighed to his knees.
But no longer within his past he desperately searched.
And, like gold, gradually begun to recover love, life and worth
Within his heart's heaviness.

Hail's prophecy

Earlier in the day there was hail; Rapidly escaping
the heights.
Like a messenger of some type of prophecy I could not
foretell. And, with a violent crash, the ground broke it's
flight. Then the crystals melted into the surroundings.
Those that hadn't yet left the sky, within the clouds,
kept soaring; Smashing into others which were none-
stirring.
Then they created rushes of electricity, as they, like
figurines,
danced & spun; Illuminating the clouds in bolts of
lightening.
Each bolt sending rumbling vibrations through the air;
Bouncing
& echoing off the earth before reaching our ears. After
we
witnessed their dance, lighting up heaven's lair, and
striking
the ground like spheres! Finally came the rain;
Nourishing
& cooling the earth & animals on it which roamed. Only
from the destruction came life and abundance with the
downpour.
As neither were born to dance alone!

Bull by the horns

Unaware of her anger and
her fear,
In her life she was just a mere
passenger,
Unable to harness her passion &
her power.
Instead they controlled & consumed
her,
In her state of frustration, youth &
immaturity.
So, with the handbrake up, she was
stuck and unfree; Driven rather
than being the driver.
Until, one day, upon gazing at
herself in the mirror,
She overcame her stubbornness.
Then, gradually, reclaiming the driver's
seat, forwards she charged!
And In her anger and her fear she
no longer stood tall,
After she had tamed her inner bull!

# Rooms of her Soul

In limbo, she roamed the corridor of the hotel,
past the many rooms; Tired and weary.
Through their windows into them she could see
clearly.
However, stalked by fear, she was unable to settle
or sleep,
And from room to room she would crept,
As, one by one, their locks were forced & their glass
shattered,
Until none were safe in which she could shelter.
Desperate, to another corridor she wandered.
Soon, she came across a room that, despite being
new, she felt a
strange connection to...
Sat on the bed, suddenly she began to feel safe &
unburdened
with doubt, and, in it's place, felt a calmness.
Finally, she was then able to rest.
For, it's occupant she felt as if she knew...
And through the glass barriers, by which she was no
longer divided,
Not just her own, but, through their eyes she could
see,
And of her strength & courage she was reminded!

# Into the Desert

In the desert he stood.
His gaze resting upon the horizon,
where he witnessed the flood,
In a faraway kingdom; Once rich in vegetation,
But, by the tide, it's reeds were swept away, and
destroyed was the foundation on which they lay.
For, it's king, powerful, had claimed the land
By building a castle,
But foolishly made it out of sand!
His people wished upon a star,
But their dreams instead settled & built up in the
clouds,
Unable to ascend very far;
Only hovering above the land in which they prowled.
Driven by greediness,
They had an endless thirst,
But, by the waters, they were drowned instead of
nourished.
The gates that separated their
empire burst,
And beyond their land the waters ventured,
Eventually reaching the desert; Quenching it's
dry sand and earth.
And the desert, that once was dry and bleak, became
prosperous
As, by the flood's waters, rivers and oceans
were created,
Where, eventually, it's people fished.

Winter's worth

In the Winter, she searched the field alone.
Whilst the rest of the animals slept; Looking
for her seeds below a tree, that, on it's branch,
rested her home, and where in the Summer
they'd collect. But they were now hidden beneath
a thick, white layer of snow & frost. For, it was
unfortunate, she pondered, but was just what
Winter brings. Although the little bird couldn't help
but question at what cost? Nevertheless, she knew
she'd have to leave her bitter cold homeland, or, would,
through hunger, become weak, & her journey South she
would not be able to withstand. And so, not long after,
she left her home, & on her voyage she started.
But it wasn't long until Summer came back around,
& she flew back East, where she once again began to roam.
She was surprised to see the same seeds from last year,
beneath the snow, which had by then melted. Except now
they had sprouted, and begun to grow! As, by the blanket
of snow, they had been protected from Winter's harshness,
& when, by the sun, it had vanished with an abundance of
water they were nourished! For, it was then that the little bird
knew of Winter's cost; Without it the true worth
the sun would be lost.

Faith and Trust

Tired from walking, she came across a garage,
Where outside she rested.
Alone and in need of lifting, a clairvoyant she
began texting, as night slowly
set in. But In void of answers, into the garage
she ventured.
After gradually reclaiming her strength and
energy,
That had, amongst the vehicles and bits of
scrap metal, in the garage been
stored and buried,
She was ready to make her way home.
However, aware of the darkness, she didn't
want to journey it alone, so she
decided to call on her guardian,
As, in her heart, she became less stubborn,
Upon examining what she had already built
and woven. For, she then knew that it was
enough.
Now, in the Angels, It was time to hand over
her faith and trust.
Grasping it's strong wings, she held on tight,
as across the heavens, on
it's back, she began to ride.
And, just like a brand new car, she felt
restored and re-energized, as she
followed the light,
With a clear view of her destination In sight!

I am an ocean

I am an ocean.  I am deep. Sometimes
warm, other times cold;
Forever changing.
As brisk as the rapids. Sometimes I'm close,
While other times I
flow distant from the shore.
I can be calm & steady, but wild & erratic;
Smashing into the rocks against the coast,
Unwilling to let you step inside me.
Yet as strong as the current that pulls you near,
and sucks you under;
Way down to my dark, murky depths. But, as
the wind sets in,
you will be lifted to the surface & carried
back shore,
Where you will once again be safe. For, I am
an ocean, with it's
strong, powerful & willing force. That will never
stop flowing,
And rising from the depths!

Ego

Within our ego do we hold true knowledge?
Or are we, at times, by it misguided?
Were Adam and Eve really deceived?
Are we, & everything, truly all that we
believe?
Is this truly reality?
Or, rather, only how we believe & wish it to
be?
The ego; Resulting in & the culprit of
judgement and
discrimination,
From the apple which led us to question.
Instead of living in faith, love & purity,
We gave way to our need for knowledge
in our vanity..
Not real wisdom, just a false illusion!
For, in our hearts, truth we already know,
but it is our
ego that leads us to forever question!

# Volcano

Standing afar, I watched it erupt:
Spewing out hot rocks & lava.
The people below, terrified, frantically tried
to escape to shelter. But no sooner
were they, by it's vengeful fist, struck,
As their cries pierced my ears.
But, around my chest, I wore a heavy shield of armour.
Yet stood tall from off the ground;
Towering over it's thistles & thorns.
From here I know I must now depart,
Or face forever being bound.
For, cursed was this place and all in it that duelled.
Afterwards they'll say that it was a shame,
But I refuse to be blinded by it's hell!!
They'll declare that even in it's wickedness there was
still potential growth in its
grain. Although I never seen it embraced by the sun.
For, as it's feeble, withered hand reached out,
Only by it's harsh heat would it be overcome.
For, now new life will surely spring from it's ashes,
As replenished shall be this land.
And it's grain shall be sturdy & long, so that even from
the heavens it won't be
missed.
And, 'behold', the sight that shall instead be reaching
out shall be grand.
For, blessed shall soon be the promise of this land!

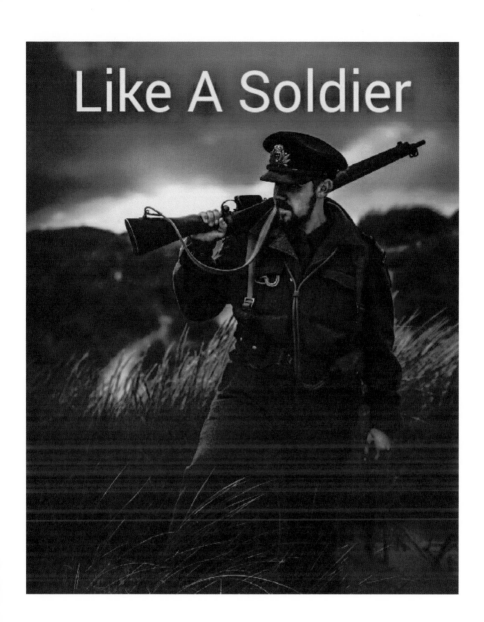

Like A Soldier

First, let them not be plagued by hunger".
Said the Soldier, when asked about his wishes
for the people of
of the future. Secondly, let them have warmth
and shelter,
And no more greed, hate, fighting and fear.
In it's place, let them have love, morals, and
values.
In order for men to be good men, first give
them the
opportunity to live as people, rather than exist
as
animals!
For, one or all of these basic needs will ensure
that
they prosper,
And one day be a good soldier"!

Crucifixion without resurrection

Chained & bound on this earth,
He started out submissive in his pain.
A crucifixion, yet without resurrection,
Or rebirth
From which to rein.
Judged by the people, a wannabe prophet
& saint he became,
Though leading not to a rise, but a fall,
With a crown of misguided pride & gain.
In embracement, he stretched his arms out wide,
But had blisters on the souls of his feet
From his chosen path, from which he could not
turn his back & hide,
And the resentment that he could not fleet.
Tired & worn, he bared the thorn,
Till his worth he could argue & prove no more.
For, different, so felt condemned since the day
he was born. As
well as his own, it was their sins which he wore.
And, In the end, acceptance & love he bought,
But not with truth, instead lies & fear.
So satisfaction he never sought.
And, so finally, into his heart, it was him who
plunged the final, fateful
sphere!

Morning fog

It was dawn when it restlessly began to
hover.
After the Spring &
Summer.
Drawn to the river, which was cool &
deep.
On it's surface it then
settled & gathered,
As, in hibernation, the animals were
sound
asleep.
Absent from the sun's heat, and before
the bitter
snow, It's intensity
then further magnified, as it departed
from
the river below.
The true colours of the leafs could be
seen,
amongst it's murky atmosphere,
Where transition was keen, and where
beauty
understanding in it's nature was clear.

The wonder of winter

In winter it can seem so bleak.
The flowers and wildlife retreat,
While the earth sleeps.
But amongst the seemingly gloom,
There is change at loom...
Even In the darkness there is still a
sense of wonder.
For, nature never falters, but,
Instead
daydreams & ponders.
And by Spring is rested and fonder!

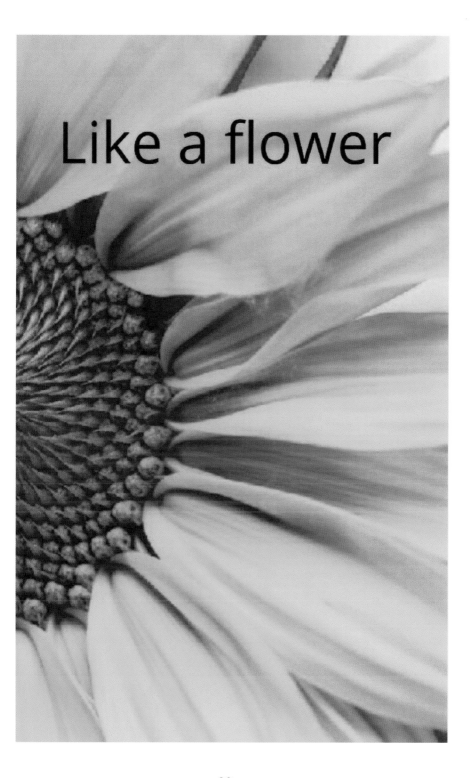

Like a flower

Life isn't always a sunny
picnic, that much I
know!
But whenever I see a
dark cloud up ahead I do
not run for shelter.

Because, like a flower,
sometimes we need a
little rain,
in order to blossom and
grow!

# Law of the jungle

He wanted it all,
But, in the end, he had to settle,
when, in
Arrogance, he no longer stood tall,
As, from his pedestal, he took a tumble!

For, when it's your happiness before others
that you choose
always be prepared to lose.
Because the real secret to lasting success
is to always stay
humble,
And live & work together in harmony.
Thus, It's the law of nature, & the law of the
jungle!

Arrest of her heart

It was late in the evening when she heard the first knock;
A man claiming to be from the red cross,
Holding a donation box.
But, disinterested, she slammed the door, as to his kind she was wise to;
They were mostly scammers she knew.
Although rather than fading his persistence grew,
And again he knocked on her door.
Reluctant, she answered it.
However, she soon discovered that he was a burglar! As he pushed passed
her & into her house; Knocking her to the floor!
For, of many of her possessions she did not much care,
Except that was for one,
And her love for it was quite rare.
Panicked, she knew she was alone!
She banged on her neighbours doors, but none of them were home.
So towards the town, to the nearest phone box, she ran like lightening! So far
was the journey that darkness soon set in.
After dialling the police she alerted them of her intruder,
Then set out on her journey home,
With only one street light to guide her.
However her mission became in vain,
As she found herself lost,
& the path leading her home she could not regain.
Until she caught sight of a familiar face;
A person from her past whom had once treated her cruelly,
But, bizarrely, her anger was erased;
She smiled at him and in return on the right track he assisted her.
Arriving home, she saw her street, that was deserted, now full of her
neighbours; Gathered outside of her house, whilst, with the sirens of the
police cars, daylight once again stirred.
To her relief the thief was arrested,
& nothing, including her much loved possession, was taken.
Rather In it's place found that she had gained wisdom,
After, by what seemed to be a greater authority, her faith was tested,
And, In her heart, resurrected.
No longer did she then find herself isolated,
But, instead, in mercy, she was reunited.

Righteous

Righteous is the seed in which
hatred is planted,
And where blame &
judgement is rooted.
Where you are, in pride,
blinded,
And where no growth &
wisdom is sprouted.
Righteous is the shallow sea in
which no life is founded,
&, by the sun, is shrivelled
instead of nourished.

# Her gyspy soul

Placing flowers in her hair, the
flamboyant Gypsy, amongst
nature, sat freely, without a care,
While up and down the path of her
consciousness she curiously leapt;
Confident, yet mindful of every
step. Graceful in the way she
carried her mind, body & soul.
Completely & equally at one with
them all, she was balanced &
whole,
And, as she faced the world, in
control!

# Time and lesson

Time does not exist,
Only in our universe.
Beyond that, it is endless,
With no end or beginning,
Just constant transitioning,
Within another dimension,
Where everything is beyond our comprehension.
And where this life is merely an illusion;
A realm and a gateway which leads to another,
Someplace in which our understanding and awareness
is higher.
Here our mind tries to comprehend what our soul
already knows,
In our everlasting quest for answers and knowledge.
To reconnect with a source and our true selves we have
been in a constant bid,
Ever since the time when we were first given knowledge,
And formed in a creator or creator's image.
The finishing touch upon completion,
Before being cast from the garden of Eden;
It's womb,
Into life and creation.
At present, like time, in our awareness we are someplace
in between,
A place which is neither any known hell or heaven.
For, if it weren't for this then there would be no purpose
within our soul's journey or lesson.

Unchanging

That which never changes is real.
Although our earthly body perishes
our soul, that which we truly are, is
eternal.
For, that which can be defined is
not real,
as, there is neither a beginning or
an end;
Just an forever expanding.
The soul can not be restricted or
closed in.
What it longs for the most, it's
driving force behind it's quest
for knowledge,
light & happiness, is freedom &
space,
so that it may be free to stretch out
& to with the
universe & infinity,
That in which it is, embrace!

Live

What is the definition of life?
To LIVE without fear,
so that you may be free to create
and manifest your dreams and desires.
You are only ALIVE when you are
truly happy and In the presence of love.
Love is at the core of true fulfilment.
The perfect definition of love is
truth, light and goodness.
The opposite of love is evil and hatred.
EVIL is LIVE spelt backwards.
For, it is fear that is at the root of,
and what is behind, evil and all that is
bad.
And, so with fear there can never
be truth or life!

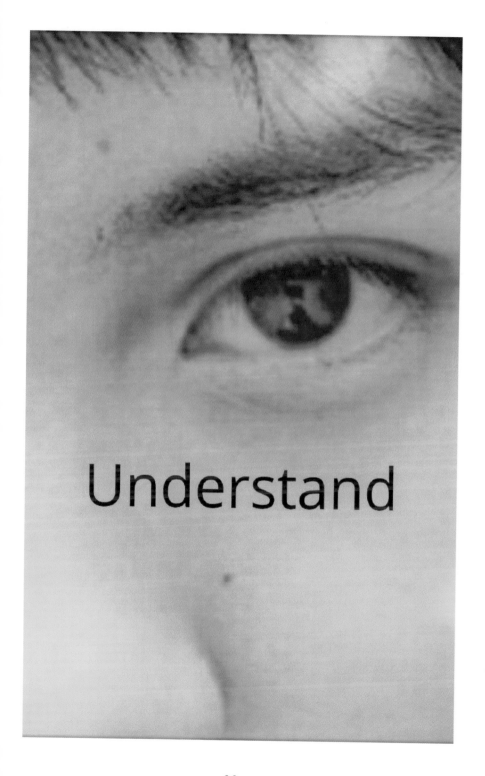

Understand

Don't judge or try to change me.
You haven't walked in my shoes,
Lived my life,
Or had my upbringing.
For, neither were you born with
my
personality,
That, together, gave me my unique
understanding & perception!
It is that which divides us, and that
which
makes you, who you are,
And what makes me, who I am.
So, rather than judging one
another,
Lets try to understand!

**END.**

Printed in Great Britain
by Amazon